"WILL YOU MARRY ME ...AND BE MY MOM?"

by Mark Giersch

FIRST EDITION, 1989

ISBN: 0922352-02-X
Library of Congress Catalog Card Number 89-063132

Cartoon Illustrations done by Travis B. Skinner

DEDICATION

A book of light-hearted humor for adult children of alcoholics and adult children of trauma. This cartoon book pokes fun at the many unspoken facts, truths, myths, and coping mechanisms of growing up in a dysfunctional family. It is intended to help support persons who have experienced the pain of rejection, loneliness, sadness, shame, guilt, and isolation by adding a touch of humor to an otherwise bleak situation. It is also designed to encourage individuals to laugh at themselves and realize, in such a tough spot, that "I am not alone."

FAMILY TREE

GRANDPARENTS

MABEL

CRITICAL
PASSIVE
CONTROLLING

JONATHAN

WORKAHOLIC
EMOTIONALLY DISTANT
HAD ALCOHOLIC FATHER

PETER

WIMPY
BASHFULL
CONTROLLED

JOAN

INDUCES GUILT
CONTROLLING
MARTYR-LIKE

PARENTS

MITCH

ALCOHOLIC
WORKAHOLIC
EMOTIONALLY DISTANT
HAS RAGE OUTBURSTS

JANE

CONTROLLING
INDUCES GUILT
DEMANDING
PERFECTIONSTIC

CHILDREN

BRIDGET

PERFECT CHILD

NORBERT

LOST CHILD

SADIE

SCAPEGOAT

RALPHY

MASCOT

"WILL YOU MARRY ME...
AND BE MY MOM?"

"DO YOU, JANE, TAKE MITCH, HIS PARENTS, GRANDPARENTS, AUNTS, UNCLES, BROTHERS, SISTERS, FRIENDS, CO-WORKERS?"

"SEE? ITEM NUMBER TWO SAYS THAT YOU CAN'T TALK ABOUT THAT."

"WE'RE FREE OF YOUR MOM AT LAST."

"CAN I HAVE YOUR PERMISSION TO FIGHT WITH MITCH?"

" SHE WANTED MITCH TO HAVE SOME THINGS TO REMEMBER HER BY."

"MITCH DOESN'T LET PEOPLE
GET TOO CLOSE..."

" NO, I'M SORRY, YOU CAN'T STAY HERE."

"OH HONEY. YOU KNOW YOU'RE THE ONLY WOMAN IN MY LIFE."

"YES, DEAR, OF COURSE I TRUST YOU."

"IT'S FRIDAY. IT'S MY TURN TO TOUCH YOU FIRST."

"WELL, MAYBE THEY'LL SHRINK."

"I WON'T COME OUT UNTIL YOU
STOP ACTING SO CHILDISH."

"IF YOU GET UP AND GO TO WORK,
TONIGHT YOU CAN HAVE TWO MARTINIS."

"MAYBE A FOOTPRINT WILL WORK."

"THAT'S IT. YOU'RE GROUNDED."

"I'VE ALWAYS WANTED TO BETTER MYSELF."

"SAY YOU LOVE ME."

" SURE, BOB I'D BE GLAD TO HELP. . .
I'LL SEND JANE RIGHT OVER."

"YOU CAN TRY, BUT HIS FAVORITE
PROGRAM IS ON."

"AND SO, AFTER A LOT OF DATING, I FINALLY FOUND ONE SICK ENOUGH TO MARRY."

"UH-HUH, SURE. I'M INTERESTED
IN EVERY WORD YOU SAY."

"WE'VE DONE A GREAT JOB OF BONDING."

"DOES THIS HAVE A LIFETIME GUARANTEE?"

"THIS IS MY BEST FRIEND."

"NOW IT'S OFFICIALLY A RELATIONSHIP."

"MY DAD TOLD ME I SHOULD GET SOME."

"I BROUGHT A FEW THINGS FOR YOU TO TAKE ON VACATION."

"YOU WON'T BELIEVE THIS, BUT YOU'RE
THE ONLY PERSON I CAN TALK TO."

"BESIDES OUR MARRIAGE, WHAT ELSE CAN WE BLAME ON HER?"

"MOM FORGOT MY NAME THIS MORNING."

"I REALLY DON'T LIKE THE TASTE. I JUST DO IT TO GET HER ATTENTION."

"I'M NUMBER FOUR. I TRY HARDER."

"ISN'T THAT CUTE? RALPH'S FOLLOWING
IN HIS FATHER'S FOOTSTEPS."

"AND NOW MOM AND DAD, I'LL MAKE IT DISAPPEAR."

"HE'S HERE TO HAVE HIS RAGE REMOVED."

"I HOPE HE DOESN'T USE THIS AS AN EXCUSE NOT TO MOW THE LAWN ON FRIDAY."

"NO, NO, YOU ENTER. JUST KNOWING I'D WIN IS GOOD ENOUGH."

"DEAR LORD, THANK YOU FOR PROTECTING
ME FROM ANY BAD HABITS."

"LOOK, MOM, THERE'S YOUR NAME."

"SOME DAY THIS WILL BE YOURS."

"DAD, I JUST CAN'T REACH YOU."

"I COULD JUST NEVER SAY GOODBYE."

"EVERY TIME I COME HERE, I GET A
STRANGE FEELING."

"I WANTED MOM AND DAD TO NOTICE ME."

"IT'S OVER NOW. MOM AND DAD HAVE STOPPED FIGHTING."

"NORBERT HAS A HARD TIME SAYING GOODBYE."

"BUT MA, THEY DIDN'T NOTICE ME."

"OH GOOD. I THOUGHT I WAS LATE...
HAVE THEY STARTED FIGHTING YET?"

"WHY DOES SHE GET ALL THE ATTENTION."

"THAT'S THEIR WAY OF SAYING,
'I LOVE YOU.'"

"I'M READY FOR THAT TALK NOW."

"DON'T INTERRUPT. I'M TEACHING
THEM HOW TO COMMUNICATE."

"SIGN ON THE DOTTED LINE."

"OKAY. IT'S TIME FOR OUR
FAMILY CONFERENCE."

"HONEY. I THINK OUR COMMUNICATION
IS IMPROVING."

"TWO BITS, FOUR BITS, SIX BITS, A DOLLAR — PLEASE DON'T LET US HEAR YOU HOLLER."

"CAN WE PRETEND?"

"MY FATHER AND I ARE VERY ATTACHED."

"I WONDER WHAT SHE SEES IN HIM?"

"I WONDER WHY BRIDGET LETS HER
BOYFRIEND RUN OVER HER?"

"HIS MOTHER GAVE ME THESE WHEN WE WERE MARRIED."

"FOR MY NEXT TRICK, I WILL BRING
ABOUT WORLD PEACE."

"AFTER YOU FINISH THE WADSWORTH PROJECT, YOU CAN GO OUT AND PLAY."

" STAY AWAY FROM DAD. HE LOST THE
WADSWORTH SALE."

"I HAVE TO GO. IT'S MY TURN TO WATCH DAD."

"CAN'T YOU DO BETTER THAN THIS?"

"YOU CAN'T GO OUT UNTIL YOU EAT ALL OF YOUR FOOD."

"WHEN I WANT MY MOM'S ATTENTION,
I OPEN THIS DOOR."

"WHAT DO YOU MEAN, YOU THINK THERE'S SOMETHING DIFFERENT ABOUT MY FAMILY?"

"I JUST LOVE THE BIG, STRONG, SILENT TYPE."

"I'M LEAVING IF YOU KEEP TREATING
ME LIKE THIS. I MEAN IT."

© 1988 by MARK G.ERSCH

"BUT SADIE, IT'S A FAMILY TRADITION."

"WHENEVER MOM AND I FIGHT, WE GO SHOPPING TO MAKE UP. WE USUALLY FIGHT RIGHT BEFORE I HAVE A BIG DATE."

"NOW THAT I'VE CRIED, YOU'RE SUPPOSED
TO GO BUY ME GIFTS."

"BEFORE I GO OUT WITH SOMEONE, I WANT TO FIND OUT IF THEY'RE SUITED FOR THE JOB."

"I WON'T GO OUT WITH HIM BECAUSE
HE'S SO NICE... GENTLE... KIND...
ER... I MEAN BORING."

"NO, I CAN'T TONIGHT. I'M ALREADY BOOKED."

"YES, IT'S IMPORTANT TO TALK ABOUT IT.
I'LL PUT YOU DOWN FOR 7:00 - 7:05 p.m.
NEXT THURSDAY."

"AFTER YOU READ SO MANY, YOU CAN WRITE YOUR OWN."

" FOR YOUR PENANCE..."

"DAD AND I MADE A DEAL... IF YOU YELL AT ME ABOUT THE CAR, I GET A NEW BIKE."

"HEY KIDS— COME IN HERE AND
GET ON THE TABLE."

"GO AHEAD. I PAID GOOD MONEY
FOR YOU TO YELL AT HIM."

"YOU ALWAYS HAVE TO BE DIFFERENT, DON'T YOU?"

"I KNOW SOMEBODY WHO NEEDS
SOMEONE LIKE YOU."

"YOU CAN NEVER HAVE TOO MANY OF THESE."

"SOMEDAY, SON, YOU CAN OWN ALL THIS
SEX APPEAL."

" TRY THESE ON FOR SIZE."

"OH, YES, I KNOW WHAT IT IS. WE'RE ALL ON THAT AT MY HOUSE."

"WHY DIDN'T YOU TELL ME THIS WAS
A COSTUME PARTY?"

"OH MOM, DON'T APOLOGIZE.
WHAT'S PAST IS PAST."

"DUCK! HERE COMES ONE OF DAD'S DEFENSE MECHANISMS."

"WHY ARE YOU READING THAT THING?
I ALREADY TOLD YOU WHAT TO BE."

"WHY NOT? IT WORKED FOR DAD."

"YOUR LIFE WILL BE A TEST OF
THIS MATERIAL."

"WHY CAN'T WE GET TO EACH OTHER?"

"WHAT DO YOU MEAN? WE HAVE A LOT OF REASONS TO STAY TOGETHER."

"SHE'S BEEN ACTING UP LATELY."

" DON'T WORRY. IF YOU GET A DIVORCE,
YOUR FATHER WILL MARRY YOU!"

"HIS CHOICE IS, STAY SICK OR I DIVORCE HIM."

"I DON'T WANT YOU HERE ANYWAY."

"DO YOU THINK MOM IS TRYING TO
TELL DAD SOMETHING?"

" I SEE YOU PACKED ALL OF YOUR
IMPORTANT STUFF. "

"IT'S AMAZING HOW WE FOUND EACH OTHER."

"IF YOU CAN'T OBEY THESE, I CAN'T MARRY YOU."

"OH YES... I'M GLAD YOU'RE STAYING FOR DINNER."

"WILL YOU MARRY ME . . .
AND BE MY MOM?"

"THEY MUST BE AN AWFULLY CLOSE BUNCH."

"FINALLY, A CHILD THAT BELONGS TO ME."